Sibling Poets

Travels Through Two Lives
Fairy Path to Ha-Ha

Jenny Bradley
and
Jonathan Bradley

THE CHOIR PRESS

First published in the United Kingdom in 2021 by

The Choir Press

ISBN 978-1-78963-184-5

Jenny Bradley is a writer with a successful career in business. She writes in a variety of genres. A published poet and short story writer, she recently won an award for flash fiction. Her radio plays have been broadcast on the BBC. Writing has been published in anthologies, websites and in the Bristol Post where she was columnist for a year. Her literary agent obtained an offer from a publisher for her first novel.

Jenny loves writing and has written creatively for a lifetime, both to reflect on experiences and for the simple joy of it. Travelling alone round the world for seven months in 2007–2008, blogging http://jennysworldtripno1.blogspot.com was a way of recording her experiences, keeping in touch and making sense of what she was experiencing. She now lives on the North Somerset coast. Jenny reads at events, is a judge for Poetry on the Lake and a Director of The Clevedon Literary Festival.

Jonathan Bradley has been writing and reading poetry from an early age. This is his third book of poems to be published. The first two were of poems inspired by butterflies: *Papiliones* (Choir Press, 2017) and *A Kaleidoscope of Butterflies* (Merlin Unwin, 2020). His poems have been included in several other books, and he has made a number of public readings of his work at literary events. He has also contributed articles to *The Countryman, This England,* and *Atropos*, among other magazines and periodicals. He is a Director of The War Poets Association. Jonathan divides his time between Bristol and the Languedoc in southern France, and has travelled widely during a varied professional career. He shares a love of the natural world and the need to care for it with his sister, Jenny.

Contents

For our Parents

For Jenny's children, Lindsay and Louise and her grandson Charlie

For Jonathan's children and grandchildren

Introduction

When the two of us were playing with Dinky Toys and squabbling over Lego in the warm sunshine of southern France all those years ago we might never have imagined that we would be publishing a joint selection of poems as grandparents. Here it is. Our lives may have followed different paths but we have both written poetry from time to time, and have perhaps surprised each other by addressing similar themes, albeit in varied styles.

Our parents might have been less surprised, not only because of a natural confidence in the potential of their offspring, but because books, story-telling and word-play were important in our family life. These early experiences helped shape our tastes and sharpen our perceptions. Early seaside visits gave us a keen attachment to Cornwall in all its wildness and charm. Travels with our parents in Europe, through France, Spain, Andorra, Italy, Austria, Switzerland, Germany, Luxembourg, Belgium, Norway and elsewhere turned us into young cosmopolitans.

The poems in this book are arranged in pairs, in each case one of Jenny's and one of Jonathan's, roughly following the chronology of our family's lives, from beach holidays when we were toddlers, through the moves of our parents to America, France and Belgium and then back again, to middle age, their decline and eventual death. Along this road, in our different ways, we contemplate our love of the natural world and of the sea, the passage of time and its effects on our mental and physical being, our travels, hopes and griefs. Short notes before each pair of poems help to put them in context, but they should largely speak for themselves. One special pair of poems considers siblinghood in all its complexity.

As we started work on preparing the final text we were overtaken, like the rest of humanity, by the horror of the Covid-19 pandemic. We make no apology for referring to this in our poems, as it will change the world whatever its ultimate outcome. We like to hope that there will be a greater nurturing of our planet; an appreciation of nature's value. A permanent change where humanity's role becomes guardian and travelling mate of the natural world, an integral and supportive one which may save or even ensure mankind's future.

In the case of each of us the poems are just a selection of what we have written. We now both think of ourselves as writers, though we have pursued very different careers in other respects.

We hope you will enjoy reading these poetic reflections, which may in one sense be personal but should have a wider resonance for many people.

Jenny Bradley
Jonathan Bradley
2020

We were taken to Cornwall from being small children. This sparked in both of us a continuing love affair with this magical county, particularly the coast. Jonathan always loved body boarding in the surf, until at least five of his toes had gone numb. Jenny wore wet suit, shoes and gloves, but always refused to wear a surfing hat.

Daymer Bay
by Jenny

Sunshine sits on my shoulder
The glint of sea behind
That whole big sky, blue
As waves curl in gentle bubbles
And weed wanders with the tide
Shells shift and pebbles rock
Back and forth

The gulls wheel, calling over our heads
Another food source spotted
A potential victory for survival

As sand sifts through my toes
I sieve my soul, I catch my dreams
I watch waves wash with me
As life settles

The resting space carved in sand
Will disappear with the tide
Comfort now
Warmth of sun beaming on the beach
A drift of sleep
A catch of thought
A pleasant murmur
A girl, a boy, a dog
Today's joy
Right next to me
Right now.

Breakers
by Jonathan

From smooth to rough, they burst
in artless effervescence
to end their long long run,
a voyage from nowhere to nothing
in Kynance Cove.

These swellings of the wide ocean
erupt into a few seconds
of dangerous beauty,
their curling crests
wasted on the west wind.

On the cliff the turf is still and calm:
none can put their backs to the waves,
and breakers hold our gaze,
each of us safe on the salt-sprayed cliffs,
and entranced by the passion of the seas.

Up here a scent of blue and silver,
from the forcing, rushing thrust
that is swallowed time without end
by rocks that never tire
but only splinter now and then.

Never are the waters still,
but the restless waves give us rest -
a strange and turbulent serenity,
and we are astonished by peace
under a pure smooth sky.

Living in France as children had a huge impact on both of us, not least because we became bilingual. The family lived first in Marseille, a violent city in the 1960s. It was the era of the French Connection drug runners and of the Algerian Crisis, when bombings and shootings were quite common.

The Golden Lady is on the top of the Basilica of Notre Dame de la Garde on the hill above the city. For Jenny, the love of sun and coast became a theme throughout her life. Her poem reflects the effect of the coast on our souls and the sadness of seeing our beaches polluted.

Au Bord de La Mer
by Jenny

Les vagues m'embrassent
Nuages, petits choux-fleurs
Flottent au ciel
Dansent comme des marionnettes,
Chassent le vent.

Souffle, souffle.

Le parfum d'algue m'hypnotise
Une ceinture ramassée par la plage
Appuyée sur mon Coeur
Quel dommage que c'est
Une poubelle en plastique.

Mais, toutefois
La joie dehors,
Aujourd'hui,
Quelle douceur,
Gentille mer
Quelle ivresse.
Le sourire du soleil
Est le chauffage de mon âme.

Marseille
by Jonathan

When Protis the Phocean Greek
married Gyptis, Ligurian princess
he gained a wife, and a hill.
The Massilian creek became a new port,
and then the old;
southern light and limestone heat
boiled up a bouillabaisse
of peoples of the Middle Sea:
Congers of Barbary,
Scorpion Fishes from the calanques,
Gurnard netted by leather-skinned fishermen.

Pompey sailed in with the dusty Sirocco,
his legions with scorched Saharan sand on their boots;
Caesar left on the cold Mistral
a city still barely French
for another thousand years.

Foreign Legionnaires marched from their forts,
neck-shades streaming,
from a city pulling on its ancient moorings
on the eastward drift.

They subdued places and peoples
even more foreign:
Arabs, Berbers, Touaregs, Moroccans,
who lounged in the alleys
while forgotten prisoners listened
through the cell-bars of the Chateau d'If.

Dealers in powdered fantasies
made their French connections here,
and wreakers of terror
loosed their plastic bombs.

But throughout,
the scent of empty crab shells,
salt and thyme in the nostril,
an evening meal of creamed cardoons
with aïoli and fine chopped fennel:
a sea-wolf supper for sea wolves.

Now the floating yacht club diners eat
the fish that swam beneath them hours before.
The number 83 bus patrols the Corniche,
its head-scarved passengers
averting their Islamic gaze
from David's naked form –
a Jewish hero sculpted by a Christian,
and a mystery to Muslims.

After two years living in Marseille we moved to Paris. Jenny went to the International School in Paris whilst Jonathan was sent to boarding school in England. From then onwards we saw each other only in school holidays.

Our genes bind and shape us. Our mother read prodigiously and our father loved poetry. Perhaps it is not surprising that their two children have written this book together.

Sibling Love
by Jenny

Wrenched away at six.
My playmate.

Golden days outside,
The cherry tree swing,
Or cars
Round and round the dining room table.
You were gone.

A lifetime lived apart
There, but not there.

Families flew by
Husbands, wives, came, went,
Pulled and pushed us
Stretching our binding thread of spider's silk.

Round the world I went, alone
'it was like part of me was missing'
You said, on my return,
Your arm, flapping.

We stood together at our parents' grave,
Threw red roses on the headstone,
Neither wanted to think
Who was next.

A Brother and a Sister
by Jonathan

If I'd been born a girl
would I have been you?
And if you'd been born a boy
would you have been me?

Why did I have the Y
and you the extra X?

The answers were in ancestors
long gone.
Perhaps they asked the same questions,
and knew no more than we do.

Here we are, the two of us,
often chalk and cheese:
the genes were jumbled,
more mixed than matched.

Yet generous Muses gave us
a rhyming gene,
so our nature urges us to versify
with no great purpose
but to entertain.

The family move from 1960s Paris to Durham was a major culture shock.

In 'Soft Washed Moors' Jenny remembers those of Durham, Yorkshire or Scotland and childhood picnics with parents. There always seemed to be a random friendly dog. Jonathan wondered what it would be like to be a sheep. The individual in his poem perhaps recalls the unconventional streak running through the family.

Soft Washed Moors

by Jenny

Soft washed moors
    Heather purpled
Air billows through pockets of grass
    Rainbows star each blade
As dew dropped
    Competes with the sun's rays
Eerie call of a curlew
    Makes the lapwings rise
    Black and white dancing
        Wind tossed swooping darts

The brown beck chuckles then
    Runs deep through peat
Rubbing sides to pick up pigment
    Tea leaves down the water pipes

And as night huddles into hills
    Tweed colours gentle to grey tones
Low cold swirling mist settles
    To disguise the day 'til dawn.

An Individualist Sheep

by Jonathan

She was the contrary sheep,
invisibly different;
normal sheep should follow,
offer themselves as meek meat
with a helpless bleat,
but she went her own way
to the far side of the field –
a sheep's continent away
where the grass was no greener
but it was her grass
with a fine view of the obedient flock
in the hollow below,
a grave departure from sheep custom;
she was suspected of woolly thinking
and wilful unsheepfulness.
She had the rare distinction
to die of old age.

The poem 'Time' while nominally about nature is a reflection of our lives. In 'Carpe Diem' Jonathan writes about time's different moods. He has always found it difficult to wake up in the morning, whilst Jenny is a night owl.

Time
by Jenny

A bubbling brook
   Sparkling, busy
Clear pure motion

   Suddenly
A giant shunt of earth
   water muddies to sludge
Sticks eddy, clog, lump,
   little whirling pools of scum froth, go nowhere fast
Stuck,
waiting,
'til bigger bundles bulge and burst

   A torrent of terror
Out of control
   A log, a puppet, a pawn
      Marooned
         Waiting

thrashed down
in crumbling
crashing
disaster.

How long 'til the water runs smoothe,
Calm, gilded, winking in summer sun
Serene and steady,
Comfortable within its wooded walls?

Carpe Diem
by Jonathan

They carp on about it –
seize the day!
Sometimes you can seize it
with decisive hands.
Sometimes the day squirms away
though your fingers clutch at it,
and other times you cannot *see* the day
and even if you could
you wouldn't want to seize it.

Mondays are fast and slippery
dodging this way and that
past the bedroom door –
slithery carping days

Tuesdays, sometimes full of grace,
are often tainted by Mondays,
still slimy but slower.

Wednesdays are middling days,
neither one thing nor another:
woeful, they try to strive and only cope.

Why seize Thursday
when you can hope for Friday?

The days that surprise, when lovers kiss,
are Fridays, and like the child,
are loving and giving
and should be cuddled.

Saturday comes with handles and grips
convenient straps and finger-holes.
It can be held close and squeezed.

But Sunday seizes *you*,
like its child, bonny and blithe, good and gay
unless church pews or shopping
darken its joy.
Carpe hominem et mulierem!

Poetry is a journey into the imagination, and we have both enjoyed the mystical and magical. Jenny's poem, although not written when her children were young, was written for 'children and all adults who believe' about a secret path with fairies …
Jonathan's poem is about a small butterfly native to the Balkans, and its two names form the title. The meeting of its two personae is almost a fairy story.

The Fairy Path

To be found, by children and all adults who believe, between Six Ways and the Sea Front.

By Jenny

I walk the fairy path
To the salty sea
Each day it's different,
It depends what I see.

Have the fairies been
Out on the town
Picking new snowdrop hats?
Or finding flat mushrooms
For picnic mats?
Or making new
Swirls and frills
For party dresses
From daffodils?

The big beech on guard
Shakes a leaf if there's trouble
Doesn't want
No hubble and bubble.

I sometimes hear a whisper
A rustle right here
But when I step to look
The fairies hide in fear.

I think I found a house once
In the bottom of the tree
A quick glance and I saw fairies
Not one – but two – no three!
But quickly, like a lightning flash
They flutter and they fade
Softening back into their
Shady hidden glade.

I'll be back again tomorrow
Hunting the fairy queen,
But if I don't find her
I'll just enjoy the green
And I know that I'll find
    – If I look –
Enough evidence of fairies
To write a whole book.

Balkan Pierrot and Little Tiger Blue

by Jonathan

High in the Albanian Alps
Pierrot escapes his melancholy,
so far removed from Columbina
that he cannot see her flirt with Harlequin
and so need not despair.

His white face peppered with the Balkan sun,
he craves a mirror
to discover if he still can smile,
and gazing on the glassy water
of a mountain pool, he sees no clown.

A tiger, quite as shocked as he, looks back:
'don't take fright', the tiger says,
'my roar is very small
and I never use my claws'
so Pierrot is assuaged and changed.

His tail aloft he bounds away a cat,
to stalk his prey:
a wide-lipped rictus grin;
until he looks again into the pool
and acts once more his comic role.

Looking back, life rushes by whilst objects perhaps change more slowly but they are witness to the world. In 'Tide and Time' Jenny imagines joining the tide under the pier watching time passing.

For Jonathan, time flies by and each tide seems faster. 'The Joy of Gravel' was written for some of his grandchildren who discovered its delights at the seaside in Cornwall. It hardly seemed long since their parents, his own children, were playing in a similar way.

Tide and Time
By Jenny

I watch from below.

I can see up skirts,
Watch bloomers and red satin knickers.

Now I hear the rumble of a pushchair
The clump of a toddler's trainers
The chase by the parent.
See the bag of the fisherman thump down
Watch the butt of a rod rammed between planks
A twitch if a fish bites
A writhing net when it's caught.

I lie with the tide
Make love with the waves
Caress the sinewy limbs of the pier
Feel rocks and sand under my back
Send seaweed squelching and swirling round metal
I am here and I am gone
The smell of salt and the unruly pull
Of the waves.

The Joy of Gravel
by Jonathan

For happiness, paradise, gravel is best,
as long as it passes the grandchildren test;
Rebekah and Jago and Isla all know
the places to find it, and that's where they go.

The middle of pathways where people must walk
will certainly not make the little ones baulk,
and <u>there</u> is their favourite – it's gravel in mud,
the sort that's washed down by a heavy rain flood.

Oh gravel, oh gravel of purest delight
goes further when thrown from a very great height:
it splatters and scatters all over the lawn
that gardeners have toiled at till nightfall from dawn.

A favourite with naughtiest terrible twos
is gravel concealed inside Mum and Dad's shoes;
when parents are cursing and howling with pain
well then it's the moment to do it again.

Imagine the bliss of your very own pit,
with diggers, conveyors and quarrying kit –
a heaven of gravel, unqualified fun,
the loveliest toddler-place under the sun.

A sandwich with extra fine gravel to crunch
is obviously much more exciting for lunch,
a gastronome's treat that's exceptionally grand
if liberally flavoured with plenty of sand.

But very young lovers of gravel should know
there's somewhere they'd wisely not let gravel go –
a nappy with stones in will not only smell,
it's shockingly grating and painful as well.

If, little ones, revel in gravel you must,
please <u>don't</u> make your parents excessively fussed:
however annoying their negative rants
it's not to be eaten or dropped in your pants.

Our many childhood travels with our parents through Europe in the back of their purple and white Triumph Herald and rather flash black and white Hillman Minx convertibles encouraged us both to explore the world in later life. Jenny's piece, about her travels in Cambodia, is an excerpt from the blog she wrote during a seven month solo trip round the world 2007–8. Jonathan's poem recounts his experience at Angkor Wat in the same country some years later.

Cambodia March 2008[1]
by Jenny

I fly in so early that I fall asleep as we come in to land, missing the view of all the temples and ancient buildings from the window seat I'd requested.

The road in from Siem Reap airport passes modern hotels, though many have a Khmer twist – a little uplifted portion of the roof sticking up and out at the edges. It should have been a short ride to town; however my hotel-arranged taxi went a circuitous route and then demanded 40% more than the arranged fee, because 'the price of petrol had gone up'. Querying this in the hotel, they shrugged and told me to pay the driver. Not the best start.

At 830am I hire a tuk-tuk, the wonderful two wheeled, open-air, rooved carriages, pulled by a motorbike, that seat, at a push, four people. I ask to see the floating village on the lake. We bump endlessly down an unmade road past stilt houses and one room shacks made from a frame and palm leaves, where whole families eat and sleep. Huge lorries churn up red-brown dust, presumably making a proper road, as we totter and veer at an angle along the heavily sloping edges. We stop at a police shack to buy a ticket for the boat – it is state run and you need permission from them to go as well as a US$20 fee. Everything is in US dollars – even the cash machines dispense dollars instead of the local currency, the riel.

---

[1] Blog address http://jennysworldtripno1.blogspot.com

Eventually we get to lots of boats and a melee and mayhem of people, coaches and stalls. My driver beckons me forward – apparently I am to go on a boat alone! It would seat about 20 people, but it is state run and I presume it is ok; there are plenty of other tourists around doing the same thing. As we push off a young man jumps aboard, introducing himself as Joss. He has a certain wild look about him as he flicks his hair back from his face. As we pass the floating school he explains he does this in the morning and goes to school in the afternoons, but that he is one of the lucky ones. At the end of the trip he asks me for a tip. So he wasn't included in the price!

The floating villages are fascinating. One is Vietnamese and one Cambodian. In the river on the way we pass fishermen up to their waists in water standing with nets in hand. They could have been there in any century. It is the same with the villages, although there is some power from motors. A whole community of fisherfolk live here, farming crocodiles as well as fishing and running various floating cafes cum shops for tourists.

We bump back to Siem Reap and this time head for Angkor Wat, the purpose of my trip. It is huge and slightly scary, giving off an aura of a bygone era which you catch a whiff of down the long corridors, echoes of countless human labouring lives building, marching, worshipping in their tens of thousands. There remains some stench of power, of huge misuse of humankind and a driving force that comes from some very alien culture.

I fend off the hordes of children 'madame, madame, just a dooolllar' they cry, the adults who surround you pushing their hands and arms across your tuk-tuk with guidebooks and bags and water … Under intense pressure I am browbeaten by a woman begging me to buy her guidebook, which I don't want. Of course not to want it is the best bargaining tool, and I get a $28 guide book, which they are all selling for ten, for 7 dollars. Helpfully, I find later, it starts at page 9! I view it as giving to charity and feel slightly less guilty about the price.

The general advice seems to be to either buy from those trying to help themselves, or give something concrete if there are no goods to buy, eg a meal. I didn't haggle over the price of a CD of music performed by a group of landmine victims, who were performing on the path to Ta Prohm.

Ta Prohm is a temple that has been left much as it was discovered – ie with trees growing all through and over it. For this reason it is particularly charming, nature softening the severity in comparison with some of the other temples and their bleak, streaked dark stone. It is highly popular and has been used for film sets. On the way out I stumble across a young man with a small portfolio of water colours. There is an air of despair about him and he does not try very hard to sell. He is too easy to strike a bargain with so I buy two, and wish later I'd bought more – they are very beautifully drawn, simple scenes of local life and the temples.

As soon as I can I acquire a Khmer scarf – red and white check – which I wear over my mouth and nose against the dust. I wonder if I am beginning to get the slightly feral look I have noticed about some travellers.

I visit more temples and finally ask my driver to take me to get some photos. I want to photograph the stilt houses over the river. He takes me to two grand modern homes. No I explain, the houses by the river. He realises I am actually interested in the people and stops for me. He then pulls over to the side of the road, picks up my rucksack and asks me to follow as he walks along a dirt path. I am a little unsure, where is he taking me? But we are still close to the road, there are plenty of children around and one comes up on a bike – my son he says. I follow him and he shows me the outside of where he lives and introduces me to his wife and children. His house, no more than about 12 feet x 12 feet, is built from palm fronds, which cost 2 dollars each he tells me. I give him a big tip at the end of the two days – maybe he does this with all tourists, maybe not. All I know is he needs the money a lot more than I do.

Angkor Angst
by Jonathan

Before dawn at Angkor, Vishnu waits,
six arms uplifted not enough to wave
to six hundred serenity-seekers
with digits on their digitals
by the lily-covered limpid lake;
frogs escape the Angkor rush hour with a plop
and the backpackers' flip-flops
stick in the holy royal mud.

It's a soggy, steamy dawn
click click click, plop
squelch, squelch, click, plop
plop click click click click
"Madame, you want scarf? Have your size."
"Sir, picture, very nice?"
"Sir, sir, Tuk-Tuk later?"
"Madame, scarf? Madame, coffee?"
click click plop squelch.

Vishnu has seen it all,
Vishnu is unmoved,
Most of the great moving crowd are unmoved
but they have their photo
of the calm serene moment
when they tripped on a Coca-Cola can
and caught a whiff of Marlboro
on the morning zephyr breeze;
but King Suryavarma's Karma
will live long long after
the pictures fade.

Our parents bought a house in England, Mary's Acre in the Cotswolds, when they left Durham to move to Belgium, returning a few years later.

It became the family hub and refuge until they moved in 2008.

It sat in almost an acre. They didn't name it, although coincidentally Mary is both a family name and Jenny's middle name. About one third was a wonderful old orchard.

We each brought our children for birthdays or rituals like the autumn apple picking.

Jonathan's latter memories of Mary's Acre are from well into middle age, trying to work out what that meant.

The Old Apple Tree
By Jenny

I lie under the old apple tree
Eyes half open
Quick movement in the greenery
A flit so fast I can't catch it.
I hear a thin piping, then a slight scold.
Above me settles a pale rounded belly
A petite neat bird
With startling black moustache.
Another pecks a branch above
One, two, three, four maybe,
A family of coal tits
Call and feed and flee to the hedge.

A twinkling flash flies across the deep blue sky
Twin-winged, a masterclass of delicate lace
Settles atop the lavender, looped.

The shadows dance and tease.
My eyelids droop
In the summer breeze,
As soft dreams settle.

Middle Age
by Jonathan

When there was still hope
it was worth striving
even for certain failure
aspirations were a burden
weighing down the day
and cluttering the night
but to find the doors locked
was almost a relief
there was a tempting keyhole
but I did not have the courage to look
for the chance of reassuring disaster
a little faintheartedness
was so much easier
the heavy oak of mediocrity
the fine walnut of sloth
and the bamboo slats
of false compassion
caged me
and at last I had to face
desperate comforting ordinariness …

By the time our parents left Mary's Acre, below, to live in a retirement village they were in their 80s. There was no ha-ha there, but there is at Jonathan's present home, and he started wondering about his own approaching old age.

Mary's Acre

by Jenny

Those sun kissed days
    A dove grey old stone house
Wisteria covered windows
    And leaded panes
A crumbling terrace
    Gentled by green tendrils
Open to the southern sky.
    It baked.

From babies they crawled
    Ate leaves and laughed at dust
Fat fingers clutching sticky sandwiches
    Sun hats wedged down.

As grandma snoozes under a striped umbrella,
A toddler trundles a trike
    Round and round
    Rams into the table, laughs.

A preparation for a wedding
School friends gather
A repeat visit later when
    One bolts from her too young husband.

A shelter when we needed it
    No home but that
Until jobs could be found,
    A house bought together.

A large woody spider
    Spindly, she scuttled
    Across the red quarry kitchen tiles
'Wash it with milk' my great aunt said
    'That's what we did in the pub'.
We never really knew her younger days
    – Never really asked –
But a flavour of a hard life
    Scrubbing floors in a Bristol hostelry.

Every year we'd apple pick,
    Why does it always seem so sunny?
The long handled cutter,
    So difficult to manage,
The children with their
    Short fat legs shoved into short red wellies
Picking up the fruit,
    Bruising fingers blue with blackberries
And complaining when tired.

In spring, a show of daffodils
    Month after month
Different clusters of clouded yellow
    Some with orange middles, some not,
Or frayed edges, or double blooms,
Or pale and ghostly yellow faces
    Bobbing, falling round each apple tree.

We gathered there
    Drawn to the family hub
The certainty, the censure and support
    The welcome and the cat.
The endless cups of tea,
    The answer to everything.

The kitchen floor got carpet tiles
    The walls began to crack
The roof had to be replaced
    The garage started to subside.

The stairs got harder to climb
    A stair lift was installed
The steam from endless showers
    Lifted the flowered wallpaper.

And yet my soul knows
    That sunny house and terrace
Still exists,
    Sings in our hearts on dull days
And comforts with its presence
    When nurture's needed.

Down by the Ha-Ha
by Jonathan

When I'm going ga-ga,
it won't be very far-far
to shuffle to the Ha-Ha
by the moo-moos and the ba-bas
for a chuckle and a ha-ha
at impending final ta-ta.

I'll sing a little la-la
to remember vanished ra-ra,
and sitting on the ledge
by the softly swaying sedge,
move closer to the edge
of my life.

After moving to a retirement apartment, our parents' health declined. When they died it left a big gap and a quiet telephone.

They both drank a lot of tea, and may have owed their long lives to its beneficial effects.

Grief
By Jenny

I am a sheet of water inside.
A waterfall
A flooding bucket
A bottomless ravine
Filling,
Filling.

There are no sides to climb.
I can't grip
No handles
Sheer and wet
Slippery.

I find my temper
Tucked under the sofa.
I take it out, shake it softly, smooth it down
Rub it gently.
Ready for use again.

One Last Cup of Tea

by Jonathan

Please stay a while, a little while,
for one last cup of tea;
it's difficult to raise a smile
but soon you will be free.

A parting that we can't avoid –
the day has come, it's near;
but then we're going to feel the void
and that is what we fear.

So many things unsaid, undone;
we didn't hear, we didn't look,
and there'll be silence when you're gone
the phone then off the hook.

So, stay a little longer, if you will
for just another word,
and then we'd like you to be still
and go when we have heard.

Our father had a stroke in the early morning after his 90th birthday party. He'd gathered family and friends, ordered champagne, sandwiches and cake. He stood and gave a speech. We lost the father we knew with the stroke. It was painful to see a fine mind gradually and irreversibly deteriorate. His body followed six months later, just before Christmas.

Jenny, a great tea drinker in the family tradition, wrote 'Lace My Tea' at this time.

Lace My Tea
by Jenny

Lace my tea when I get old
With quiet painless poison
Don't let me keen and cry
Don't let me want to die.
Put quiet painless poison in my tea
When I get old and my body fails
Or my mind is long since gone
Please put quiet painless poison in my tea.

Prostheses for Sale
by Jonathan

In the window,
legs waiting for bodies
hands waiting for arms
hairless heads
and body parts unknown.

In the street,
bodies waiting for legs
arms waiting for hands
heads wanting hair
and body parts unknown.

And in the shop
a healer and builder
of incomplete bodies
unable to complete
damaged minds.

There are days in our life when we are reluctant to get up, for many reasons, good and bad, as in Jenny's 'November Morning'.

Similarly, Jonathan's sonnet dates from when he commuted daily in the 1970s from Finsbury Park to Moorgate in the City of London. Sometimes he would have preferred to have stayed in bed.

November Morning
By Jenny

The soft grey pillowed light
Streaks with pink,
Birds stretch their wings
Preen flight feathers
Fly for a breakfast berry.

Lights snap on
Blanks of gold against the lifting sky.
Rumble of a stop-start lorry
Clatter of bins thrown back in drives
Whine and grind of engine.

Silence again
Broken only by the occasional lilt of birdsong.

The click of the kettle,
Whisp of steam rising from my mug of tea
I pull my dressing gown tighter,
Head back to the warmth of my duvet.

The sing of the central heating, pumping
Warmth through groaning pipes,
The chill air moving over,
Accepting the day change.

The stripes behind the venetian blinds grow brighter
The swish of tyres on tarmac
Becomes more frequent.
I rub my eyes, stretch,
Put my feet slowly back into slippers.

Sonnet: Commuter Train
By Jonathan

A magic creature like an armoured eel
Emerges from the gloom of fading night
And as it clatters closer turns to steel;
Its single eye becomes a glaring light;
The monster's flank disjoins from every gill,
Discharging travellers at the waiting line,
Amorphous shoals of dense planktonic krill
Commingling on the edge of platform nine
The beast invades the tunnel with a bound
And morning papers rustle at the jolt
Commuters meekly hurtle through the ground
To storm the city in a dawn assault
Then eight hours later after work disperse
To start the same migration in reverse.

'Stalking Sheila' was a flash fiction competition winner, gaining an award for Jenny against hundreds of entries. The instructions were: 'write a 50 word story giving the best reason for the fire alarm going off in the middle of the night at a conference.'

Midnight comings and goings can be frightening, especially if you have a mind already troubled by other things. Jonathan's poem considers how to deal with fear in the night.

Stalking Sheila[1]

by Jenny

The smash sends a shiver down my spine. I run to my room, breathing rapidly. Peering from behind the door, I watch as delegates appear, dragging on dressing gowns.

Will Sheila and Tony appear from two rooms, or one? Phew. Two. I can sleep now, knowing there is no fire.

---

[1] See notes on previous page for an explanation of this piece.

Finding Strength
by Jonathan

If fear comes in the night
to startle you with its sudden leer,
and you catch its foetid breath
close to your face,
stare it out
bare your teeth
blow grains of defiance
into its red-rimmed eyes;
it will shrink away, but hide:
you may find it
consorting with solitude
on a bleak Saturday in May
as it slithers through the undergrowth
of a beautiful empty garden;
you may suspect it
disguised as a bank statement
and it may leap at you
from photograph albums.

But fear is craven, lusting for shame
ready always to shrink into the shadows
where it belongs;
you can scare it
with what fear fears,
the weapons of hope:
primrose petals in spring sunshine
ripples on an azure lake
moonbeams on the woodland floor
the evening's first mouthful
of good Champagne
my skin against yours
laughing after making love;
and if fear hesitates, then show it this:
our strong embrace and fearless kiss.

We both love the West Country and have lived here, within a few miles of each other, for the past twenty five years. The area is beautiful and inspirational, in all sorts of ways.

Jenny loves the idea of inanimate objects with a secret life of their own. 'Clevedon Pier' has fun with this idea.

Winterbourne is a West Country village where Jonathan knows no-one called Wendy and intends no offence towards anyone with that name. He has rarely visited Winterbourne and imagines that it is probably a lovely place.

Clevedon Pier
By Jenny

Do you take off your little green hat at night?
That pixie cap
perched on the pagoda?

When darkness cloaks
and the sea is still,
is this your moment?

Do your planks relax,
    balustrades droop a little,
do you stretch those spindly legs,
    give them a slow shake, one by one?

Perhaps you pick them up in turn
    like a giant stalking spider,
carefully place one down, then the next,
find firm sand,
stride across the channel?

Do you wander down the coast?
Peak at Penarth, have a quick canoodle with Cardiff?

Or do you simply snooze?
Take slumber until rattled awake
by clang of gates,
clatter of heels,
the bang of the doors opening.

The Wendys of Winterbourne
by Jonathan

Oh Wendys, come hither, the tennis club calls
so gather your Slazenger rackets and balls;
remember on Thursdays its nine-o-clock sharp –
be late and we'll probably mutter and carp.

When Wendys are windy, with stories to tell
they're full of their nothings and boring as hell,
conveyed from the suburbs to play on the court
in Volvos and Audis that someone else bought.

Their waistlines aren't quite as they'd want them these days
and frumpiness threatens in various ways,
with well-worn and sensible catalogue shoes,
support-bras, old anoraks, non-iron trews.

When all those around them don't know what to do
their deep-rooted Wendiness carries them through:
convention and habit help them be clear
what good Middle England should firmly hold dear.

They've Waitrose for groceries (though Tesco's not bad),
the Telegraph daily (what they've always had)
and not too much culture, it wouldn't feel right
especially as Wendys aren't always too bright.

Their husbands have probably not quite retired
although it's a year or two since they were fired;
they're Colins and Rogers and Brians, these chaps,
and all possess battered old Harris Tweed caps.

Oh Wendys, where are you now tennis is done?
Does anything else give you quite so much fun?
Will any amongst you be tempted today
to roll with your lovers in freshly-mown hay?

But Wendys are sensible, Wendys are strong
and Wendys can never, but never, be wrong;
so please do not mock them – we need them about –
they hold things together without any doubt.

Jenny has loved being in, on or near the sea since childhood. She now lives by the North Somerset coast. This has led to writing a series of coastal poems reflecting the constantly changing light on seasons, tides, weather and nature at different times of day throughout the year.

The next two poems are part of this coastal series.

'Coast' was sparked by a view of the bay when the tide was out, laying bare the extensive sand banks. The Severn Estuary has the second largest tidal range in the world; on a spring tide, over fourteen metres.

In 'God Serves Breakfast', Jenny was struck by seeing a spotlight of golden sunlight on the water and her imagination turned to food.

Coast

By Jenny

The sand lays out
Its bare ribs
Like the great carcase
Of a monster fish
Spread-eagled in the mud,
Its tail licked by
The incoming tide.

The shore, clothed in
Fingered gloves of seaweed
Reaches out to
Silk smooth water,
With sun reflected houses
Wet painted there.

God Serves Breakfast

By Jenny

Great golden bowl appears
On thick brown purple water.
God is serving breakfast
On the Severn Estuary,
Cornflakes with cream.
The cafes on the seafront
Have nothing on this iridescent sumptuousness.

Below that splattered light show,
A diving thriving whirl of silver fins,
Bouillabaisse for lunch?
He won't serve it where breakfast was.
Light, too transitory.
Follow the food, like the fish,
Where it is.

Sun is wrapped in salty wind with
Clouds at its beck and call.
Monochrome for an instant, then
Opens a new tablecloth,
Shaped on the surging tide,
Running with the water.

Catch those blustered purples and sunset shades
Before the light is caught in night's net.
Settle.
Digest.
Serene water.
Never for long.

Dinner may be served
In deep brown darkness.

Jonathan does not live by the coast but loves the sea in all its moods.

The Fishman Cometh
by Jonathan

The fishman comes on Fridays
with sea air in his van,
Ambassador of Neptune
complete with sailor's tan.

There's sea-weed on the mudguards
and just a hint of salt;
a mermaid's on the dashboard
who swings each time they halt.

But in the back the fish lie,
their eyes all dull and blank,
once trawled out from the waters
around the Dogger Bank.

The fishman isn't bothered
and just looks at the scales.
He has to sell his produce
or else the business fails.

The fish are cooked for supper,
the heads go in the bin,
a long way from the sea foam
where each was free to swim.

A Day at Trebarwith Strand
by Jonathan

When the surf is up at Trebarwith Strand
and the waves foam white on the clean firm sand,
under tattered towels are contorted limbs
of the hapless folk as they don their swims.

Then behind the wind-breaks the sun cream's smeared
in the hope that later the clouds will clear,
but their favourite sunhats are worn all day
as the grannies doze and the toddlers play.

And the roar and rush of Atlantic waves
are the soothing sounds that a tired soul craves;
with some salt on our lips and the breeze in our ears
there are reasons to live as anxiety clears.

All the pink ice creams and the mottled arms
can beguile our taste like nostalgic charms,
while the rocks and sea and the simple sky
keep the darkest tenebrous spirits high.

And there's sand in sandwiches, sand in tea
but you do not care as you're by the sea,
and your sore red nose is the price you pay
for a Cornwall seaside and surfing day.

When you load the car with picnic things
all the seagulls cry but your heart has wings;
you can still feel surf fizzing round your toes
at Trebarwith Strand where the west wind blows.

We were both fortunate to have lovely gardens to enjoy during the lockdown associated with the Covid-19 pandemic. Even though it was a difficult time, it brought us closer to the nature we have loved all our lives. It also brought reflection and frustrations, as in Jenny's poem 'Caged'. Jonathan's poem takes pity on a solitary daffodil.

Caged

Lockdown April 6th 2020
By Jenny

My daffodils grow tall.
The cowslips unfurl, reach for the sky,
Forget-me-nots speckle the lawn
As I tread, warily,
Remembering.

I breathe, feel, am.
I sense the air
Cool on my cheek,
Wind ruffling my hair,
The breath of reason,
Keeping me
In this four cardinalled space.

Apace,
I prowl up and down the edges,
Peer through picket bars,
Pause to idly watch
The birds' content,
Beaks full of twigs,
Nesting in the thickets,
Holes in the wall.
They choose their homes here.
Plants, satisfied, root and spread.
Yet restless,
I peer over the old stone boundary
And wonder where the centuries are now.

The Self-isolating Daffodil

By Jonathan

Why are you alone daffodil?
Perhaps you didn't choose to be there
all on your own, it's just that
last year a bird put you there –
so maybe you're not self-isolating.

You need not feel too lonely because
you still have the spring breeze in your petals
and visits from bees and butterflies;
the warming earth sustains your life
and holds you close.

And below that fine sunshine bloom
is a bulb that holds your memory
and will bring you back next year
maybe this time with a friend or two
to keep you company.

Two more lockdown poems. Jenny loved the peace of early lockdown and yet felt the presence of the covid pandemic raging in the background. Her poem 'Lockdown' has a sense of this together with hope for the future. Jonathan wondered what it might have been like during lockdown for the poor and needy. His poem travels to South Africa.

Lockdown April 2020
By Jenny

There is a blossom stillness
    As the day fades to pink,
    And clouds darken
Against the washed pale sky.

Outlines are silhouette sharp.
    Birds breeze their last
As indigo sucks colour from heaven.

A bat flits dark against the yellow moon,
Stark profile in a petrified night.

Shadows
Hover over us.

Plead your dreams.

Cool night air caresses
As songs fill my head,
Sweet thoughts of tomorrow.

Beyond the Gates
By Jonathan

The fillet steaks sizzle on the Braai
In the Cape Town twilight
and swallows gather by the pool
before the long flight back
to safely chilly English spring.

Beyond the gates, different fates:
in shanties, meals of tasteless millet meal
with poisonous hooch;
for all the struggle, fights for rights
their worlds are razor wires apart,
the nation's rainbow
now a tattered multi-coloured ribbon
flapping in the winds of history.

Outstretched hands and open sewer stenches
are thrust from half-conscious minds
of bull-necked Boers
by gulps of calming Pinotage
and bellies fortified with twice-cooked fries.

Women shelter under stealthy Leopard trees
as ADT patrols pass by;
impertinent baboons feed well on scraps
from gourmet restaurants,
while behind the railing bars
machetes clash for stale Mopane worms.

When the wires are breached
and spring apart in murderous whiplash;
when the electric gates swing wide,
will hands be clasped in friendship?

One wonderful element of lockdown for many, including Jenny, was the pause of human life and the greater presence of nature, previously often subjugated or destroyed by modern human living. Some days reminded her of nature's wonderful fecundity and ability to regenerate. Jonathan's poem describes a similarly languid day in Greece a few years ago during the financial crisis of 2008.

Pollen Loaded Air

June 7th 2020

By Jenny

Full loaded pollen air,
All rounded, soft,
Hangs perfumed, heavy, pregnant,
Thick and warm,
Its sweetness caresses my tongue
Like laden clover
Oozing nectar through my teeth,
Embracing fruit and field,
Raising hard green apples from fragrant pink flowers,
Licking glowing white petals to gleaming red strawberries,
Blazing rich cherry blossom into dark juicy jewels,
And heather into seas
Singing with bees.

Patates, Patates, and Death to Bankers
By Jonathan

Swallows wait on the wire
for nothing in particular
unbothered by the morning Greek sun,
Bougainvillea billows from a garden
while Stavros on his rickety veranda
looks lazily significant
at the start of a long day
of little meaning;
bees buzz close, and lavender scatters its scent
into our late and languid breakfast.

In the distance, disturbance –
A strident voice bellows through
metal-rattling speakers
worthy of a North Korean labour camp,
thin and threatening.

We pause our yogurt and honey:
in this troubled country,
where anger smoulders in the olive groves,
festers in the fishing boats
and humiliation stirs in the coffee,
has revolution begun?
Has there been a cut too far?
Was this the last olive
that broke the donkey's back?

The Tannoy voice comes closer:
confident, insistent, persistent, but calm …
we cannot yet hear the words
– too far, too foreign –
and now it's here, in our street,
a small truck with a loud speaker
laden with vegetables and fruit:
"πατατες, πατατες, μελιτζανες"
"potatoes, potatoes, aubergines."

No revolution, just business as usual,
No demonstration, just the promise
of sautéed aubergine and fresh Greek salad.

Now we are nearer the end of our lives than the beginning.

In 'How Long is a Minute' Jenny explores the relentless nature of time.

Jonathan's 'Last Swallow' shows time often moves faster than we want it to, and that we try not to think about the end.

How Long is a Minute?
By Jenny

It stretches, turns, revolves, teases.
A drop.
A long thin line.
How far does it go?

A seemingly endless dream, a moment taken,
Blinked,
Past.
A tick, or several, or tick tock,
Or, tick tock tick tock
Tick tock.

Is it finished?
Not yet
Interminable,
Full of seconds.

I catch that raindrop paused
    in rainbow sparkle,
A fine golden ray of sun
    spikes it to the window
Trapped.
How long, how long, how long?
A pause, a breath, a heartbeat, two –
I watch
Worlds collide.

Does it snap at the end, or ping?
Announce it's over?
No, it just starts again
Tick tock tick tock tick tock.

Last Swallow
by Jonathan

There will be a last time for everything:
a last time we hold hands
a last time our lips touch
a last time we say goodnight
and will we know?
Will we look forward or look back
to the last kiss?

One day, some day, will fly the last swallow
Of our end summer.

But there was a first time of it all
the first full moon over the Mediterranean
the first thrill of your hand on my thigh
and we knew then it was the first time.

How shall we know when the last time has come?

In the end the first and last will join
And we shall blend
in the Western ocean swell.

Relentless 'progress' does not always feel positive. In 'Machine is Man', Jenny looks to the future. In his sonnet, Jonathan takes a humorous glance at urban driving.

Machine is Man
by Jenny

Zombies, wandering with phones
Trip, look up, zone in again
No longer needing mobile thumbs,
Minds mapped to each machine.

One way control.

Unaware they stagger
Trained to take response
Think thought, reply,
Instant control.

A buzz in the brain
A tickling tremor, changes -
Harsh, head banging headache
With digression.

Easy.

Manipulation by machine
Domination by circuit
Instruction by instant message
Builds an electronic edifice.
Chip driven life, complete.

Sonnet: Traffic Joy
by Jonathan

You hide inside a glass and metal cage
Not strong enough to save your flimsy life,
And sometimes feel the raw red pang of rage
When drivers make lewd gestures at your wife;
They're rude extensions of their loved machines,
Inhuman as a piston or a wheel.
Such folk at home may not be cruel or mean
But stuck in traffic that's the way they feel.
Once hooting starts it fast becomes a din
As drivers shut in cabins lose their calm
And try to fight a war they cannot win.
There does remain one temper-cooling balm:
Since, if the traffic makes your patience wilt
You *can* enjoy being idle without guilt.

Sometimes there is some hope for the future as in Jenny's 'The Past and The Future'.

Meanwhile in another of his 'City Sonnets', Jonathan bemoans the delinquencies of some delivery drivers.

The Past and The Future
by Jenny

Smug sleek Tesla,
Subdued strip of leading lights
Calmly cruising, muted speed
Subtle shade of quiet slate,
Toned tyres,
Perfectly manicured.
Not a hair on your chest.

Overtaking you, for now,
A desert of aggression
Flash dash of fossil fuel
Outpouring of go-faster fumes
A supercharged velociraptor
Fleeing down the fast lane
Towards a futile future.

Sonnet: Delivery Driver
by Jonathan

He never wonders why his van is white,
A colour seen as innocent by most;
His secret load is wrapped and out of sight,
Each sender distant, cryptic, just a ghost.
He'd like to know what packages could hold,
Although outside they all look much the same;
They might contain a bomb, or bars of gold,
But either way he has the praise or blame.
He has no truck with limits on his speed
And parks wherever visits make him stop.
To yellow lines and signs he pays no heed,
In haste to make an urgent parcel drop.
But still he knows his favourite bit of fun:
To ring the doorbell, turn and quickly run.

We dream throughout our lives, an important outlet to show us our desires and pull us forward. Sometimes they are put on hold, or never fulfilled, or come true, but the act of dreaming pulls into existence something real we can relate to as part of our best existence. Jenny is keen to hold onto them. Jonathan was not born on the 29th February, but his poem describes a strange dream he had one night. Unlike Jenny's 'Dreams', his was closer to a nightmare.

Dreams
By Jenny

Dreams – where are they?
Parked in the sky
Where dreams live.

Supposing I'd been born on the 29th of February

By Jonathan

She tried to get me out on the 28th
but it was just too much
'take it easy – deep breaths,
the baby will come in all good time.'
I didn't, even though my mother tried.

I met the world on the one day in a Leap Year
you would avoid if you could,
but I didn't know
and then, of course, it was far too late.

So, when I was four I was only one
and it was a treat to celebrate
my fortieth when I was just ten.
When it was time to retire
I was still only seventeen.

And what if?
What if the years had passed slowly
According to my Leap Year clock?
When I reached seventy
everyone else would be
two hundred and eighty
and long underground.

Perhaps the world would be
an arid furnace by then;
maybe I could meet defrosted millionaires,
rescued from their cryogenic berths
in California;
or maybe see their decomposing bodies
if science failed to keep up
with egotistic search for immortality;
aliens may have arrived
in answer to foolish earthly radio calls.

Or, amazingly, things would be much the same
but I would be alone
and wishing I'd been born
on the 28th instead.

Jenny's dream of travelling alone round the world came true. She found the experience life affirming. This is her final, reflective blog entry as she returned to her native England.

During his travels Jonathan has been fascinated by the meeting of different cultures. In his poem he imagines an encounter between two great philosophers, one French and one Chinese.

Sunday, 4 May 2008[2]
Round The World
by Jenny

What have I learned from the trip? That 'hearing is not seeing' as Khaled Hosseini so eloquently puts it in The Kite Runner.

Poverty is raw up close. That there is such a thin gauze between being rich and being poor. We all have common needs but as we get more we tend to wrap ourselves in cotton wool that muffles the cries of the world's poor.

The world is also more joined up than it is easy to assume, or ignore. We are interdependent and if we don't all wake up to this soon and co-operate over the environment in particular, then man does not have a long future.

It is heartening to see that there are still pristine spots (eg New Zealand) and good to know that there is a great deal of awareness if not enough action about the environment (and sad but not surprising to see the cynical exploitation of course, everything is 'eco').

And that the vast majority of people are kind, helpful and friendly. That the world is a generous and supportive place. And a smile is almost always reciprocated.

[2] Blog address http://jennysworldtripno1.blogspot.com

When Sartre met Confucius
by Jonathan

In the blue Peacock Hall at the Astor Hotel
a philosopher sniffed a familiar smell:
from the coffee cup came the true meaning of life
with a powerful edge that was sharp as a knife.

Insurrection and protest were long left behind
and he now bravely manned barricades of the mind -
in the books of Jean-Paul he was doomed to be free,
as an existentialist clearly should be.

Though some flirting with Marx was a part of the creed,
this could only occur in an hour of great need:
true enjoyment of liberty needed Champagne -
an essential support for a French thinker's brain.

This philosopher here in Shanghai was in pain –
intellectual dyspepsia had gripped him again,
as Confucius and Sartre were mingling with Mao
and together were badly upsetting the Dao.

Now Confucius said, 'only the stupid don't change
but the cleverest also,' although that seems strange,
and he thanked his red stars that he wasn't Chinese
with his Sartrean mind in a Nauseous freeze.

The Maoists would clearly not let him be free
and Confucius would question his integrity;
so he'd sniffed at the coffee and felt rather sick –
it was time to return to some French shabby Chic.

Thematic Index

Nature

Place

Reflections on Life

Sea

Siblings

The Future

Time

Travel